ANTHONY BO

A GARLAND OF CAROLS

A HOMAGE TO BRITTEN

FOR UPPER VOICES AND HARP

The first performance of *A Garland of Carols* took place on 1st February 2006 in the crypt of St Paul's Cathedral, London, performed by the choristers of St Paul's Cathedral, directed by Malcolm Archer, with Sioned Williams on harp.

A Garland of Carols is available on the CD *My Beloved* (Guild Records 2009, GCMD 7335), performed by Oxford Voices, directed by Mark Shepherd, with Sioned Williams on harp.

Duration: c.45 minutes

The harp part (ISBN10: 0-571-52063-4; EAN13: 978-0-571-52063-3) is available separately from the publishers.

First published by Faber Music Ltd in 2010
Bloomsbury House 74–77 Great Russell Street London WC1B 3DA

Music processed by MusicSet 2000

Many thanks to Sioned Williams, who edited the harp part, and to Mark Shepherd and Ruth Massey, who edited the vocal score.

Printed in England by Caligraving Ltd

The text paper used in this publication is a virgin fibre product that is manufactured in the EU. The wood fibre used is only sourced from managed forests using sustainable forestry principles. This paper is 100% recyclable

ISBN10: 0-571-52060-X
EAN13: 978-0-571-52060-2

To buy Faber Music publications or to find out about the full range of titles available, please contact your local music retailer or Faber Music sales enquiries:

Faber Music Ltd, Burnt Mill, Elizabeth Way, Harlow, CM20 2HX England
Tel:+44(0)1279 82 89 82 Fax:+44(0)1279 82 89 83
sales@fabermusic.com fabermusic.com

A NOTE FROM THE COMPOSER

I am a great admirer of Benjamin Britten, and this work was inspired by and modelled on his *A Ceremony of Carols*, a work I first encountered during my school days. My two sons also performed the work when they were schoolboys, as choristers (or more correctly, Quiristers) at Winchester College. I had the idea of writing a set (or 'garland') of carols for trebles and harp that their choir might perform, and so I began composing again, something I not done with any great conviction since university. It took me a number of years to complete the work, mostly because I don't compose particularly quickly and didn't have much free time due to the demands of my job. But the project was certainly not helped by my desire to keep adding new carols.

Writing for harp was a challenge, and I was very fortunate to receive advice and guidance from Sioned Williams, who in fact had performed the Britten alongside my sons. The harp interlude is unashamedly modelled on Britten's, including a similar opening bass figure and its use of soft, high glissandi towards the end. It is dedicated to Sioned.

I chose to set to music some of my favourite traditional texts, including two translations: the tender 'A kiss for the baby' is translated from the traditional Portuguese carol 'Beijai o menino'. 'Cold December's winds' is a Catalan carol 'El desembre congelat', about a rose tree growing in the December snow and filling the cold air with a sweet perfume. I wrote the words to 'Lanterns' myself. In this movement the accompaniment evokes a barren winter landscape, but we are transported to a more mystical land in the middle section.

Although originally written for trebles, the carols will work equally well for female voices. I am very happy for the carols that make up my *Garland* to be performed in totality, in smaller groups, or individually.

The accompaniment was designed for harp but a piano can be substituted if this is not available, in which case the Interlude should be omitted and the following performance notes observed: the harmonics should be played an octave higher than written (page 37, bars 64–67); impractical glissandi should either be replaced with arpeggios (page 58, bars 42, 44 & 46) or shortened, starting an octave higher than written (page 61, bars 102 & 104 and page 66, bars 232 & 234).

Anthony Bolton
May 2010

ABOUT THE COMPOSER

Anthony Bolton is best known as one of the UK's most successful fund managers. For 28 years he ran the Fidelity Special Situations Fund, which became the largest unit trust in the UK. Through a city contact he met the composer Colin Matthews, who took an interest in Anthony's music and encouraged him to develop his skills. Colin introduced him to another of the UK's best-respected composers, Julian Anderson, with whom Anthony has studied since 2008. Beyond choral music, Anthony's works span a wide array of genres and include a *Fantasia* for trumpet, four cellos and percussion; *Black Sea*, a cycle of five songs for tenor and piano; an impromptu for solo harp; an octet for wind and strings; and a wind quintet. In 2010 he was commissioned to compose a choral anthem for Save the Children's Anniversary service in St Paul's Cathedral.

1. THE GLOUCESTERSHIRE WASSAIL

Wassail, wassail all over the town!
Our toast it is white and our ale it is brown;
Our bowl it is made of the white maple tree:
With this wassailing bowl we'll drink to thee!

So here is to Cherry and his right cheek!
God send our master a good piece of beef.
And a good piece of beef that we may all see;
With the wassailing bowl we'll drink to thee!

And here is to Fillpail and to her left ear!
Pray God send our master a happy new year.
And a happy new year as e'er he did see;
With our wassailing bowl we'll drink to thee!

Then here's to the maid in the lily-white smock
Who tripped to the door and slipped back the lock;
Who tripped to the door and pulled back the pin,
For to let these jolly wassailers in.

English traditional

2. THE HOLLY AND THE IVY

The holly and the ivy,
When they are both full grown,
Of all the trees that are in the wood
The holly bears the crown.

The holly bears a blossom
As white as the lily flower,
And Mary bore sweet Jesus Christ
To be our sweet Saviour.

The rising of the sun
And the running of the deer,
The playing of the merry organ,
Sweet singing in the choir.

The holly bears a berry
As red as any blood,
And Mary bore sweet Jesus Christ
To do poor sinners good.

The holly bears a prickle
As sharp as any thorn,
And Mary bore sweet Jesus Christ
On Christmas Day in the morn.

The holly bears a bark
As bitter as any gall,
And Mary bore sweet Jesus Christ
For to redeem us all.

English traditional

3. LANTERNS

Snow falls softly; lake and pond frozen,
No stars in the sky, the earth white,
So silent and cold is the night.

Let us run with lanterns
And sing sweet melody,
To see the Baby born this day
Who'll set out sad world free.

Blood red berries hang from the holly,
Thick branches weighed down where they grow,
Red berry juice staining the snow.

Light your coloured lanterns
And follow our secret trail,
Come join our band and dance with us
Across the moonlit vale.

Light your coloured lanterns
And sing soft harmony,
Come join our ship and sail with us
Across this magic sea.

Winter extends bony fingers
To touch the landscape so bare,
Our breath freezes in the cold air.

Thousands of sparkling lanterns
Light up the glist'ning sea,
We race to see this stable child
The King of Kings is he.

Anthony Bolton

4. A KISS FOR THE BABY

A kiss for the baby,
The new-born babe,
A kiss for the baby
Now giv'n to our Lady.

Shepherds run to greet him,
Follow we them,
To see there our Lady's babe
In Bethlehem.

Portuguese traditional

5. SWEET WAS THE SONG

Sweet was the song the Virgin sang,
When she to Bethlem Juda came,
And was deliver'd of a Son,
That blessed Jesus hath to name.
Lula, lula, lulaby,
Sweet Babe! sang she;
My Son and eke a Saviour born,
Which hath vouchsafed from on high
To visit us that were forlorn.
Lalula, lalula, lalulaby,
Sweet Babe! sang she,
And rock'd him sweetly on her knee.

Anon. (16th century)

7. THERE IS NO ROSE

There is no rose of such virtue
As is the rose that bare Jesu:
Alleluia, Alleluia.
For in this rose contained was
Heaven and earth in little space:
Res Miranda, Res Miranda.
By that rose we may well see
There be one God in Persons Three:
Pares forma, Pares forma.
Then leave we all this worldly mirth
And follow we this joyous birth:
Transeamus, Transeamus.

English traditional

8. COLD DECEMBER'S WINDS

Cold December's winds were stilled
In the month of snowing.
Though the world with dark was filled,
Springtime's hope was growing.
Then a rose tree blossomed new:
One sweet flower upon it grew;
On the tree once bare
Grew a rose so fair,
Ah! the rose tree blooming,
Sweet the air perfuming.

When the darkness fell that night,
Bringing sweet reposing,
All the world was hid from sight,
Sleep men's eyes was closing.
All at once there came a gleam
From the sky: a wondrous beam
Of a heav'nly star
Giving light afar.
Ah! the starbeam glowing,
Brightness ever growing.

Now the month of May was there,
Filled with God's own radiance;
Bloom'd a lily, white and fair,
Flow'r of sweetest fragrance;
So the people, far and near,
Came to see this flower rare.
O the incense wild
Of the lily child.
Ah! the scent
Of the lily blooming,
All the air perfuming.

Catalan traditional

9. TOMORROW SHALL BE MY DANCING DAY

Tomorrow shall be my dancing day:
I would my true love did so chance
To see the legend of my play,
To call my true love to my dance:
Sing O my love;
This have I done for my true love.
Then was I born of a virgin pure,
Of her I took fleshly substance;
Thus was I knit to man's nature,
To call my truelove to my dance:
Sing O my love;
This have I done for my true love.

In a manger laid and wrapp'd I was,
So very poor, this was my chance,
Betwixt an ox and a poor lamb,
To call my true love to my dance:
Song O my love;
This have I done for my true love.

English traditional

10. I SAW THREE SHIPS

I saw three ships come sailing in
On Christmas Day, on Christmas Day,
I saw three ships come sailing in
On Christmas Day in the morning.

And what was in those ships all three?
On Christmas Day, on Christmas Day,
Our Saviour Christ and his lady,
On Christmas Day in the morning.

Pray, whither sailed those ships all three?
On Christmas Day, on Christmas Day,
O they sailed into Bethlehem
On Christmas Day in the morning.

And all the bells on earth shall ring,
And all the angels in heaven shall sing,
And all the souls on earth shall sing,
Then let us all rejoice amain!

English traditional

11. EPILOGUE – THE SHEPHERDS' CAROL

As I out rode this endless night,
Of three jolly shepherds I saw a sight,
And all about their fold a star shone bright;
They sang 'terli', they sang 'terlow!'
They sang 'terli, terlow!'

Down from heav'n, from heav'n so high,
Of angels there came a great company,
With mirth and joy and great solemnity;
They sang 'terli', they sang 'terlow!'
They sang 'terli, terlow!'

So merrily the shepherds their pipes can blow.

Anon. (16th century)

A Garland of Carols

1. The Gloucestershire wassail

English traditional

ANTHONY BOLTON

Animato e energico ♩ = 132

HARP

f

5

ALL *f marcato*

Was - sail, was - sail all

10

o - ver the town! Our toast it is white and our ale it is brown; Our

mp

13

SOPRANO 1

bowl it is made of the white ma-ple tree: With this was - sail-ing bowl we'll

SOPRANO 2

bowl it is made of the white ma-ple tree: With this was - sail-ing bowl we'll

mp

16
drink to thee!
drink to, drink to thee!
f
mf
21
SOLO 1 mf
So here is to Cher-ry and his right cheek!
SOLO 2 mf
Pray
25
ALL
And a good piece of beef that
God send our mas - ter a good_ piece of beef.
ALL
And a good piece of beef that
28
ff
we may all see; With the was - sail - ing bowl we'll drink to thee!
ff
we may all see; With the was - sail - ing bowl we'll drink to thee!
ff
p

32
rit.
36
♩= 80 più cantabile
SOLO 1
p
And here is to Fill - pail
SOLO 2
p
3
and to her left ear!
♩= 80
8
p più cantabile
pp
mp
40
Pray God send our mas - - ter
3
a hap - py new year.
8
pp
43
ALL
mp
3
And a hap-py new year as e'er he did see;
ALL
mp
And a hap-py new year he did see;
8
mp
pp

* This section to be performed *a cappella* if possible.

61
let these jol - ly was - sail - ers in,
to let, to
mp
was - sail, was - sail, was - sail - ers in,
to let,
mp
64
rit.
♩ = 132
let, to let to let, to let these was - sail - ers in.
to let, to let, to let, to let was - sail - ers in.
rit.
♩ = 132
f
69
74
f
Was - sail, was - sail all o - ver the town! Our
f
Was - sail, was - sail all o - ver the town!

78
toast it is white and our ale it is brown; Our bowl it is made of the
Our toast it's white, our ale it is brown; Our bowl it is made of the
81
white ma-ple tree: With this was - sail-ing bowl we'll drink to
white ma-ple tree: With this was - sail-ing bowl we'll drink to,
84
thee! Drink to thee! Drink to
drink to thee! Drink to, drink to thee! Drink to,
88
ff
thee!
ff
drink to thee, to thee, to thee!
ff

2. The holly and the ivy

English traditional

18
blos - som
As
white as the li - ly
flower,
And
Ma - ry bore sweet
22
Je - sus Christ
To
be our sweet
Sa - viour.
The
ris - ing of
the
26
sun
And the
run - ning of
the
deer,
The
play - ing
of the
30
mer - ry
or - gan, Sweet
sing - ing in
the
choir.

34
SOLO 1
mp
The hol - ly bears a ber - ry As red_ as a - ny blood, And
3
SOLO 2
mp
The hol - ly bears a ber - ry As red_ as a - ny blood, And
3
mp
39
Ma - ry bore sweet Je - sus Christ To do poor sin - ners good.
Ma - ry bore sweet Je - sus Christ To do poor sin - ners good.
44
ALL mf sostenuto
The ris - ing of the sun And the run - ning of the deer, The_
mf
49
play - ing of the mer - ry or - gan, Sweet sing - ing in the choir.

54
SOLO 1
mp
The hol-ly bears a prick - le As sharp as a - ny thorn, And
SOLO 2
mp
The hol-ly bears a prick - le As sharp as a - ny thorn, And
3
3
mp
3
3
59
Ma-ry bore sweet Je-sus Christ On Christ-mas Day in the morn.
Ma-ry bore sweet Je-sus Christ On Christ-mas Day in the morn.
3
64
ALL
mf
The ris-ing of the sun And the run-ning of the deer, The
ALL
mf
The ris-ing of the sun And the run-ning of the
mf

69
play-ing of the mer-ry or - gan, mer-ry or - gan, Sweet sing-ing in the,
deer, The play-ing of the mer-ry or - gan, mer - ry or - gan, Sweet
73
f
sing-ing in the choir.
f
sing-ing in the choir.
f
mf
79
ALL mf
The hol - ly bears a bark As bit - ter as a - ny
83
gall, And Ma - ry bore sweet Je - sus Christ For to re - deem us

87
all.
91
f
The holy and the ivy, When they are both full
f
95
grown, Of all the trees that are in the wood The
98
S. 1
holy bears the crown. The rising of the sun And the
S. 2
holy bears the crown. The rising of the sun And the
8

102
run-ning of the deer, The play - ing of the mer - ry or - gan, Sweet
run-ning of the deer, The play - ing of the mer - ry or - gan, Sweet
(8)
106
mp
sing - ing in the choir. Sweet sing-ing in the
mp
sing - ing in the choir. Sweet sing-ing in the
(8)
mp
110
rall.
p
choir. Sweet sing-ing in the choir.
p
choir. Sweet sing-ing in the choir.
rall.
p

3. Lanterns

Anthony Bolton

20
sing sweet me - lo - dy, To see the Ba - by born this day Who'll
sing sweet me - lo - dy, To see the Ba - by born this day Who'll
23
set our sad world free.
set our sad world free.
25
mp
27
mp dark
Blood red, blood red ber - ries,
mp dark
Blood red ber - ries hang from the hol - ly,

29
Thick branch - es weighed down,
Thick branch - es weighed down where they grow,
31
mf
Red ber - ry juice
Red ber - ry juice stain - ing the
mf
34
stain - ing the snow.
snow.
♩ = 72
38 ALL mp dolce
Light your co - loured lan - terns And fol - low our se - cret trail, Come
mf
mp

41
mp
join our band and dance with us A - cross the moon - lit vale.
mf
mp
44
mf
Light your co - loured lan - terns And sing soft har - mo - ny, Come
mf
Light your co - loured lan - terns And sing soft har - mo - ny,
mf
47
cresc.
join our ship and sail with us, sail with us,
Come join our ship and sail with us,
49
largamente
f
sail with us A - cross this ma - gic sea.
cresc.
f
sail with us, sail with us A - cross this ma - gic sea.
largamente
cresc.
f

♩ = 80
51
mp
54
mf
Win - ter ex - tends bo - ny fin - gers
mf
Win - ter ex - tends bo - ny fin - gers, fin - gers
mf
57
To touch the land - scape so bare,
Our
To touch the land - scape so bare,
Our
61
breath free - zes in the cold air.
breath free - zes in the cold, in the cold air.

65
f
Thou- sands of spark - ling lan - terns
Light up the glist'n-ing sea,
We
Thou- sands of spark - ling lan - terns
Light up the glist'n-ing sea,
We
67
race to see this sta - ble
child
The
race to see this sta - ble
child
The
69
King of Kings is
he.
The
King of Kings is
he.
The
71
King of Kings is
he.
King of
Kings,
King of Kings is
he.
King of
Kings,

73
King of Kings,
King of Kings,
King of Kings,
King of Kings,
3

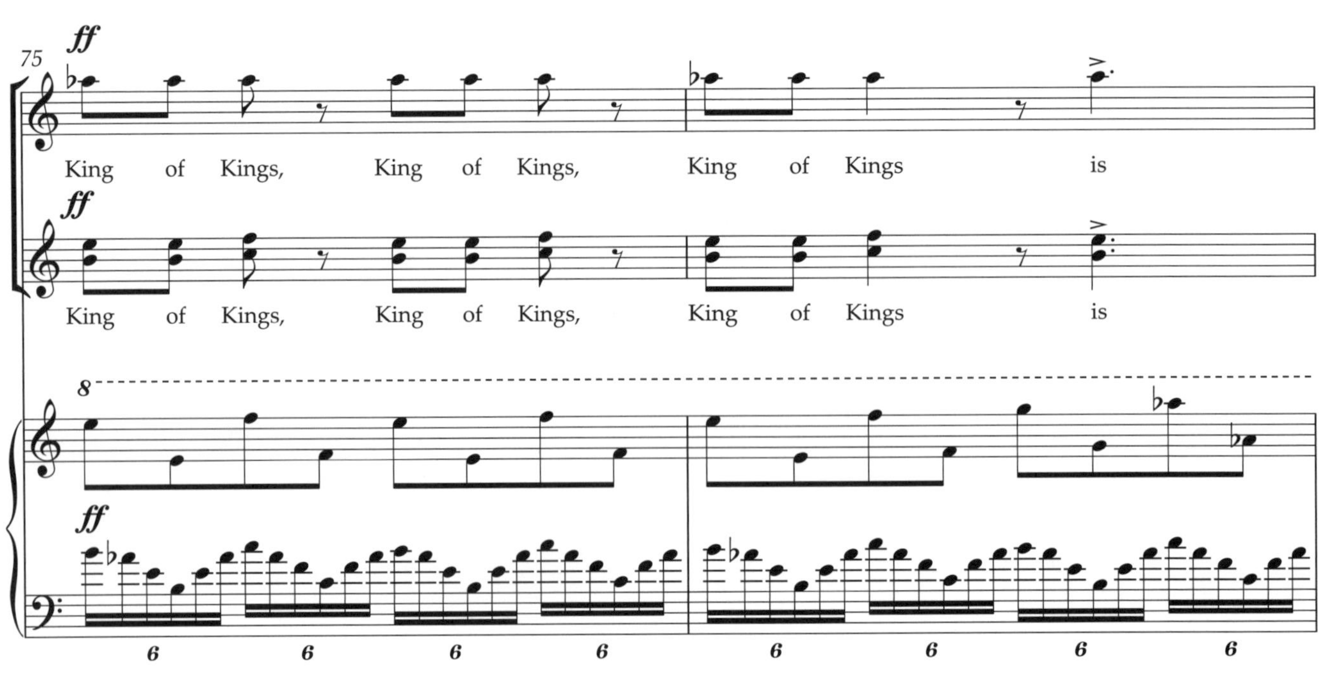
75
ff
King of Kings, King of Kings, King of Kings is
ff
King of Kings, King of Kings, King of Kings is
8
ff
6

77
he.
he.
(8)
fff
6

4. A kiss for the baby

Portuguese traditional

20
Shep - herds run to greet him, to greet him, greet him,
24
Fol - low we them,
To
28
3
see there our La - dy's babe
In Beth - le - hem,
33
3
In Beth - le - hem.
37
SOLO 2
mf
A kiss for the ba - by,
mf

44
The new - ly born babe,
A
48
kiss for the ba - by
Now giv'n to our
52
La - dy.
Shep - herds run to greet him,
56
Fol - low we them,
60
To see there our La - dy's babe
In Beth - le -
3
3

64
- hem,
In Beth - le - hem.
70
SOLO 1
mf
A kiss for the ba - by,
SOLO 2
mf
A kiss, a kiss, a kiss,
76
The new - born babe,
A
The new - born babe, born babe, born babe, born babe.
80
kiss for the ba - by
Now giv'n to our
A kiss for the ba - by
Now giv'n to our

85
La - dy.
La - - - dy.
Shep - herds run to
Shep-herds run to
90
greet him,
greet him, to greet him, greet him,
Fol - low we them,
Fol - low we them, we them, we
95
To see there our La - dy's babe
In Beth-le -
them,
To see there our La - dy's babe
In Beth-le -

100
- hem, - le - hem, - le - hem,
In Beth - le - hem.
- hem,
In Beth - le - hem.
106
rall.
p
A kiss, a kiss, a kiss,
p
A kiss, a kiss, a
mp
rall.
p
112
A kiss, a kiss, a kiss, A kiss, a kiss, a ki...
kiss,
A kiss, a kiss, a kiss, A kiss, a kiss, a kiss.
ppp

5. Sweet was the song

Anon. (16th century)

* pronounce 'lu-la' with a long 'u' as in 'cool' ** pronounce 'eke' as 'eek'

39

ff

Which hath vouch - saf - èd from on high To vi - sit us that were for -

ff

Which hath vouch - saf - èd from on high To vi - sit us that were for -

44

ff

- lorn, that were for - lorn.

ff

- lorn, that were for - lorn.

ff

meno mosso ♩. = 72

gliss.

48

p

50

p

La - - - lu - la, la - lu - la,

p

La - - - lu - la, la - lu - la,

52
2
la - - - lu - la - - by,
2
la - - - lu - la - - by,
54
mp
Sweet Babe! sang
mp
Sweet Babe! sang
56
she, And
she, And
58
2
rock'd him sweet - - ly
2
rock'd him sweet - - ly

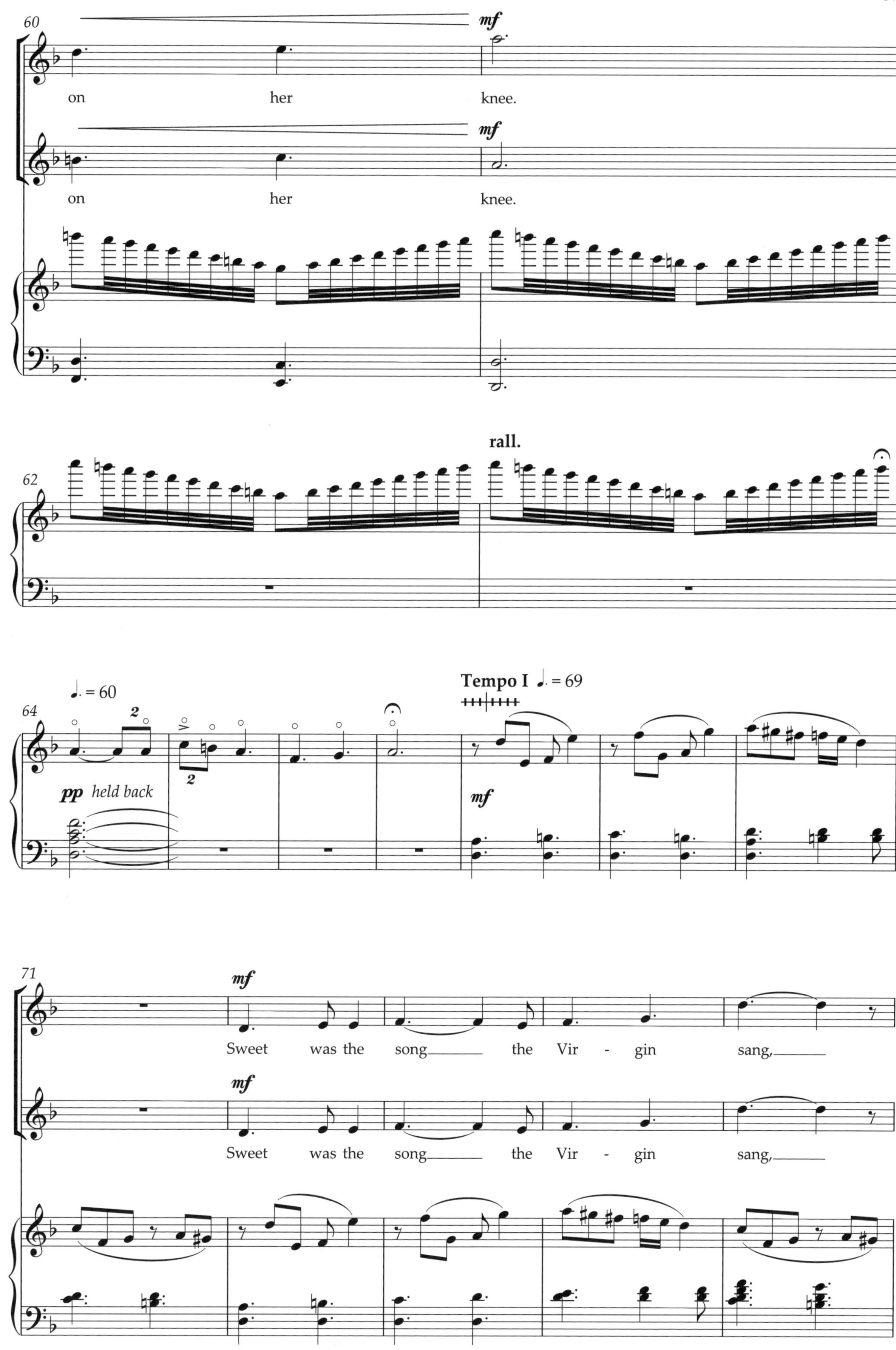
60
mf
on
her
knee.
mf
on
her
knee.
62
rall.
64
♩. = 60
pp held back
Tempo I ♩. = 69
mf
71
mf
Sweet was the song the Vir - gin sang,
mf
Sweet was the song the Vir - gin sang,

76
When she to Beth - lem Ju - dah came, And was de -
When she to Beth - lem Ju - dah came, And was de -
81
- li - - ver'd of a Son, That bless - ed Je - sus
- li - - ver'd of a Son, That bless - ed Je - sus
86
rall.
hath to name.
hath to name.
rall.
f
ff
f

for Sioned Williams

6. Interlude

(after Benjamin Britten)

19
rit.
f
a tempo
p.d.l.t.
23
p
mp
nat.
28
rit.
a tempo
f
32
p
35
f
39
p
mf
4
4
p
2

43

f *p* *f*

46

rit.

a tempo

p *cresc.*

49

mf cresc.

♩. = 35

marcato

50

f *ff*

rit.

Tempo I ♩. = 40

mf

L.H. solo

54

57

mp

60
p
65
rit.
a tempo
mf
p
pp
67
mp
pp
mf
pp
69
rit.
a tempo
mf
f
pp
mp
71
gliss.
ppp
p
74
gliss.
rit.
ppp
p

English traditional

7. There is no rose

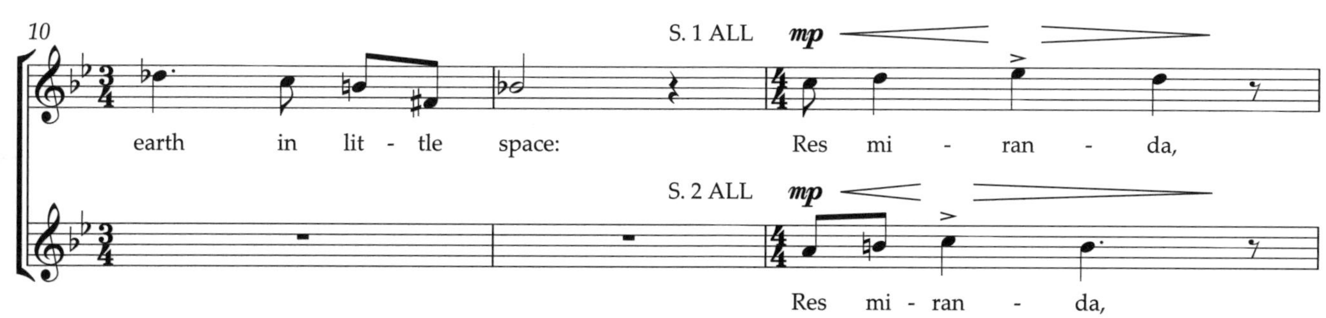

15
f
God in Per - sons Three, Per - sons Three, Per - sons Three:

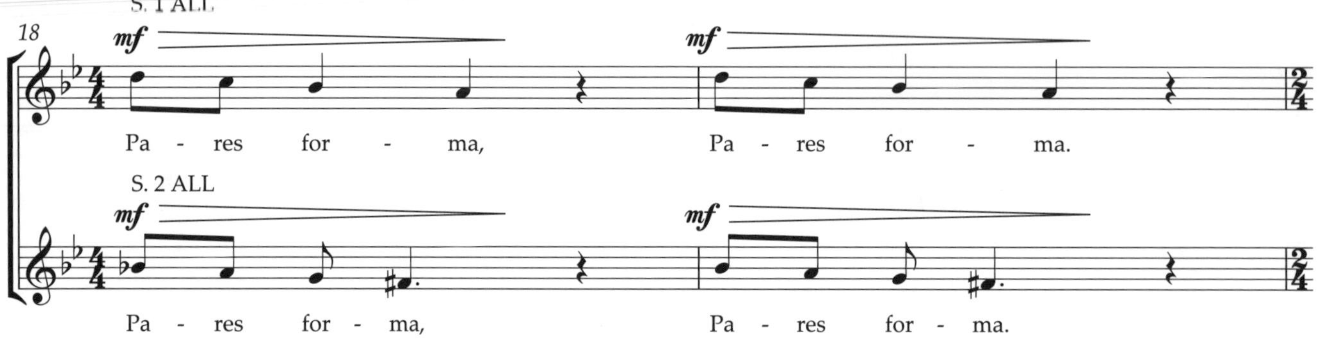
S. 1 ALL
18
mf
Pa - res for - ma,
mf
Pa - res for - ma.
S. 2 ALL
mf
Pa - res for - ma,
mf
Pa - res for - ma.

20
SOLO
mp
3
Then leave we all this world - ly mirth
3
And fol - low

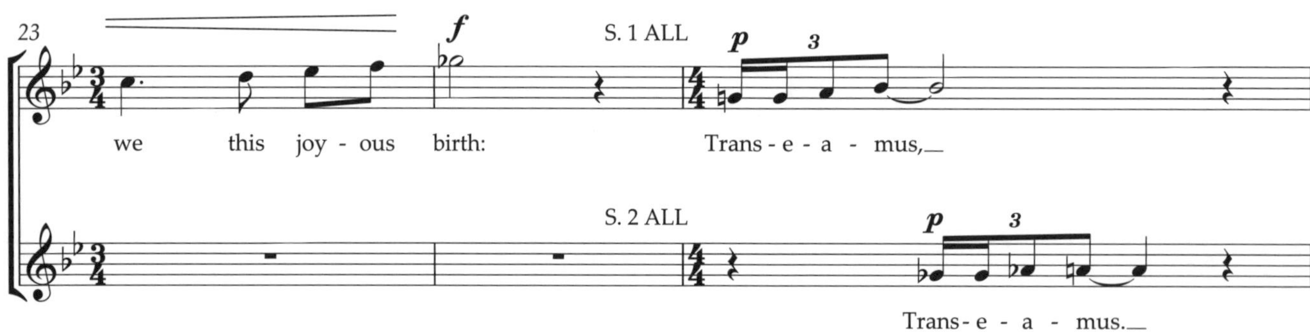
23
f
S. 1 ALL
p
3
we this joy - ous birth:
Trans - e - a - mus,
S. 2 ALL
p
3
Trans - e - a - mus.

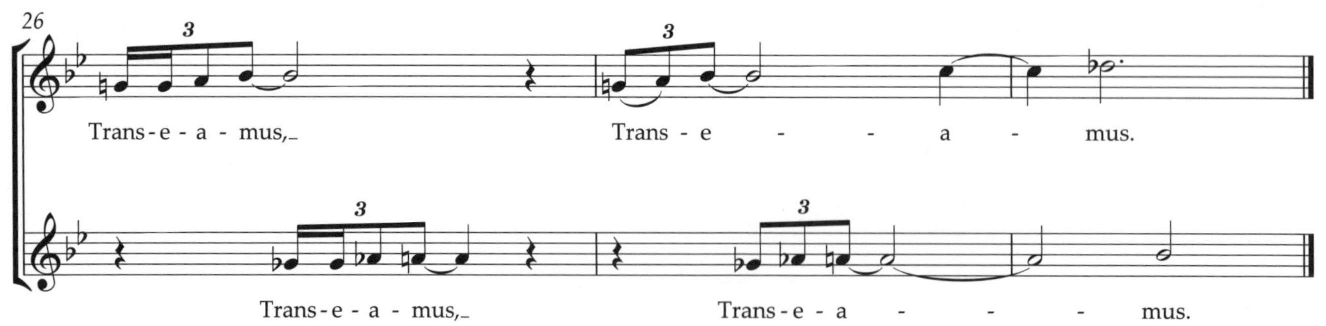
26
3
3
Trans - e - a - mus,
Trans - e - a - mus.
3
3
Trans - e - a - mus,
Trans - e - a - mus.

8. Cold December's winds

Catalan traditional

Translation of Verse 3 used with kind permission of Walter C. Ehret.

14
winds were stilled In the month of snow - ing.
winds were stilled In the month of snow - ing.
17
Though the world with dark was filled, Spring - time's hope was
Though the world with dark was filled, Spring - time's hope was
20
mp
mf
grow - ing. Then a rose tree blos - somed new: One sweet
grow - ing. Then a rose tree blos - somed new: One sweet
mp
22
f
flow'r up - on it grew; On the tree once bare Grew a
flow'r up - on it grew; On the tree once bare Grew a
mf
3

25
mf espress.
rose so fair,
Ah! the rose,
ah! the
mf espress.
rose so fair,
Ah! the rose,
ah! the
3
mf
28
rose,
ah! the rose, ah! the rose,
Ah! the rose tree
bloom - ing,
rose,
ah! the rose, ah! the rose,
Ah! the rose tree
bloom - ing,
32
p
bloom - ing,
bloom - ing,
bloom - ing,
p
bloom - ing,
bloom - ing,
bloom - ing,
3
mp
p
35
Warm and expressive ♩= 92
p
Sweet the air per - fum - ing,
p
Sweet the air per - fume, per - fum - ing,
Warm and expressive ♩= 92
pp
6

37
Sweet the air per - fum - ing,
per -
Sweet the air per - fum - ing, per - fum - ing, per -
pp
39
rit.
♩ = 96
- fum - ing.
- fum - ing.
rit.
♩ = 96
mf
43
mf
When the dark - ness fell that night,
mf
When the dark - ness fell that night,
mp
mf
47
Bring - ing sweet re - pos - ing,
All the world was hid from sight,
Bring - ing sweet re - pos - ing, re - pos - ing,
All the world was hid from sight,

51
mp mysterioso
Sleep men's eyes was clos - ing.
All at once there came a gleam From the
mp mysterioso
Sleep men's eyes was clos - ing, clos - ing.
All at once there came a
f
mf
mp
54
sky: a wond-rous beam
Of a heav'n - ly star Giv - ing
gleam from the sky
Of a heav'n - ly star Giv - ing
57
mf
light a - far.
Ah! the star, ah! the star, ah! the
mf
light a - far.
Ah! the star, ah! the star, ah! the
8
mf
61
star, ah! the star, Ah! the star - beam glow-ing, glow-ing,
star, ah! the star, Ah! the star - beam glow-ing, glow-ing,
(8)

65

rit. *p* ♩ = 92 *pp espress.*

glow - ing, glow - ing, Bright - ness ev - er

p *pp espress.*

glow - ing, glow - ing, Bright - ness ev - er

rit. ♩ = 92

mp *p* *pp* 6

68

grow - ing, Bright - ness ev - er

grow - ing, grow - ing, Bright - ness ev - er

70

grow - ing, grow - ing.

grow - ing, grow - ing, grow - ing.

72

rit. ♩ = 96

mf *mp*

76

3

mf

79
f
Now the month of
f
Now the month of
8
f
82
May was there, Filled with God's own ra - diance;
May was there, Filled with God's own ra - diance;
85
Bloom'd a li - ly, white and fair, Flow'r of sweet - est
Bloom'd a li - ly, white and fair, Flow'r of sweet - est
88
mp
fra - grance; So the peo - ple, far and near, Came to
mp
fra - grance; So the peo - ple, far and
mp

90
see this flo - wer rare, came to see this flo - wer rare, see this
near, Came to see this flo - wer rare, came to see this flo - wer
mf
rall.
92
ff
Tempo I ♩= 96
flo-wer rare, flo-wer rare, flo-wer rare. O the in - cense wild Of the
rare, flo-wer rare flo-wer rare, flo-wer rare. O the in - cense wild Of the
rall.
Tempo I ♩= 96
ff
95
li - ly child, O the in - cense wild Of the li - ly child, li - ly child.
li - ly child, O the in - cense wild Of the li - ly child, li - ly child.

99
mp
Ah! the scent, scent, ah! the scent, scent, ah! the
mp
Ah! the scent, scent, ah! the scent, scent, ah! the
mp
102
scent, scent, scent, Of the li - ly bloom - ing,
scent, scent, scent, Of the li - ly bloom - ing,
105
rit.
bloom - ing, bloom - ing, bloom - ing, bloom - ing, bloom - ing.
bloom - ing, bloom - ing, bloom - ing, bloom - ing, bloom - ing.
rit.
110
♩ = 100
pp
All the air per - fum - ing,
pp
All the air per - fum - ing, per - fum - ing,
♩ = 100
pp
6

112
All the air per - fum - ing, per -
All the air per - fum - ing, per - fum - ing, per -
114
-fum - ing, per - fum - ing,
-fum - ing, per - fum - ing,
116
mf
per - fum - ing, per - fum - ing,
mf
per - fum - ing, per - fum - ing,
mf
118
rall.
f
per - fum - ing, per - fum - ing.
f
per - fum - ing, per - fum - ing.
rall.
f
p
6

9. Tomorrow shall be my dancing day

English traditional

15
SOLO 1 and 2 mp
true love.
Then was I born of a vir-gin pure, Of
true love.
19
her I took flesh-ly sub - stance; Thus was I knit to man's na-
22
- ture, To call my true love to my dance:
S. 1 ALL
25
mf
Sing O my love, O my love, O my love; Sing O my love, O my
S. 2 ALL
mf
Sing O my love, O my love, O my love; Sing O my love, O my
mf
28
love, O my love; This have I done for my true love, for my
love, O my love; This have I done for my true love, for my

31
SOLO 1 and 2
mp
true love.__ In a man - ger laid__ and
SOLO 3
mp
true love.__ In a man - ger laid and
34
wrapp'd I was,__ So ve - ry poor,__ this was my chance,__ Be -
wrapp'd I was,__ So ve - ry poor, this was my chance,__
37
- twixt__ an ox and a poor lamb, To
Be - twixt__ an ox and a poor lamb, poor lamb, To
39
call__ my true__ love__ to my dance,__ to my dance:__
call__ my true love to my dance,__ to my dance:__

S. 1 ALL
S. 2 ALL
Sing O my love, O my love, O my love;
Sing O my love, O my love,
gliss.
love, O my love;
This have I done for my true love, for my
accel.
rit.
true love, my true love, my true love, my true love.

10. I saw three ships

English traditional

S. 1
On Christ-mas Day in the morn - ing.
S. 2
On Christ-mas Day in the morn - ing.
SOLO 1 mf
And what was in those ships all three?
On Christ-mas Day, on Christ-mas Day,
SOLO 2 mf
Our Sa - viour Christ and his la - dy,
On Christ-mas Day in the morn - ing.

74
SOLO 1
Pray, whi-ther sailed those ships all three?
S. 1 ALL
83
mf
On Christ-mas Day, on Christ-mas Day,
S. 2 ALL
mf
On Christ-mas Day, on Christ-mas Day,
89
SOLO 2
O they sailed in-to Beth-le - hem
98
S. 1 ALL
On Christ-mas Day in the morn-ing.
S. 2 ALL
On Christ-mas Day in the morn-ing.
gliss.
gliss.

106
f
And all the bells on earth shall
f
And all the bells on earth shall
f

113
ring, And all the an-gels in hea-ven shall sing, And all the souls on
ring, And all the an-gels in hea-ven shall sing, And all the souls on

120
earth shall sing, Then let us all re - joice a - main!
earth shall sing, Then let us all re - joice a - main!

127
f

134

141
S. 1 ALL
f
I saw three ships come sail - ing
S. 2 ALL
f
I saw three ships

148
in On Christ-mas Day, on Christ - mas
come sail - ing in On Christ-mas Day, on Christ - mas

155
Day,
I saw three ships
Day,
I saw three
162
come sail - ing in
On Christ-mas Day
ships
come sail - ing in
On Christ-mas Day
170
in the morn - ing.
And what was in
those
in the morn - ing.
And what was in
179
ships all three?
On Christ-mas Day,
those ships all three?
On Christ-mas Day,

186
mp
on Christ-mas Day,
Our Sa - viour Christ
and
mp
on Christ-mas Day,
Our Sa - viour Christ
194
his la - dy,
On Christ-mas Day
and his la - dy,
On Christ-mas Day
201
mf
in the morn - ing.
Pray, whi-ther sailed those
mf
in the morn - ing.
Pray, whi-ther sailed those
mf
209
3
ships all three?
On Christ-mas Day,
3
ships all three?
On Christ-mas Day,
3

216
on Christ-mas Day, O they sailed
on Christ-mas Day, O they
223
into Beth-le-hem On Christ-mas Day
sailed into Beth-le-hem On Christ-mas Day
231
f
in the morn-ing.
f
in the morn-ing.
gliss.
gliss.
ff
237
ff
And all the bells on earth shall ring, And
ff
And all the bells on earth shall ring, And

244
all the an-gels in hea-ven shall sing, And all the souls on earth shall
all the an-gels in hea-ven shall sing, And all the souls on earth shall
251
sing, Then let us all re - joice a - main! Then let us
sing, Then let us all re - joice a - main! Then let us
258
all re - joice a - main, a - main,
all re - joice a - main, a - main,
265
fff
a - main!
fff
a - main!
gliss.
fff

11. Epilogue – The shepherds' carol

Anon. (16th century)

10
3
They sang 'ter - li',
they sang 'ter - low!'
star__ shone bright;__
They sang 'ter - li',
they sang 'ter - low!'
12
mp
'ter - li,
ter - low!'
They
sang 'ter - li,
ter - low,
ter - li,
ter - low!'
'ter - li,
ter - low!'
They
sang 'ter - li,
ter - low!'
15
mf
Down from
18
heav'n,
from heav'n so
high,
Of
an - gels there
heav'n,
from heav'n so
high,
so high, Of
an - gels there

20
3
f
came a great com-pa - ny, - pa - ny, With
3
came a great com-pa - ny, a great com-pa - ny,
22
mirth and joy and great so-lem - ni - ty, so-lem - ni - ty;
f
With mirth and joy and great so-lem - ni, so-lem-ni - ty;
f
24
mf
3
They sang 'ter - li,' they sang 'ter - low!' 'ter - li, ter - low!' They
mf
They sang 'ter - li,' they sang 'ter - low!' 'ter - li, ter - low!' They
mf

26
sang 'ter - li, ter - low, ter - li, ter - low!' So
sang 'ter - li, ter - low!' So
28
mer - ri - ly the shep - herds their pipes can blow, their
mer - ri - ly the shep - herds their pipes can blow, their
30
3
pipes can blow, their pipes can blow, their
f
3
pipes can blow, their pipes can blow, their
f
f
32
pipes can blow, their pipes can blow, their
mf
pipes can blow, their pipes can blow,
mp

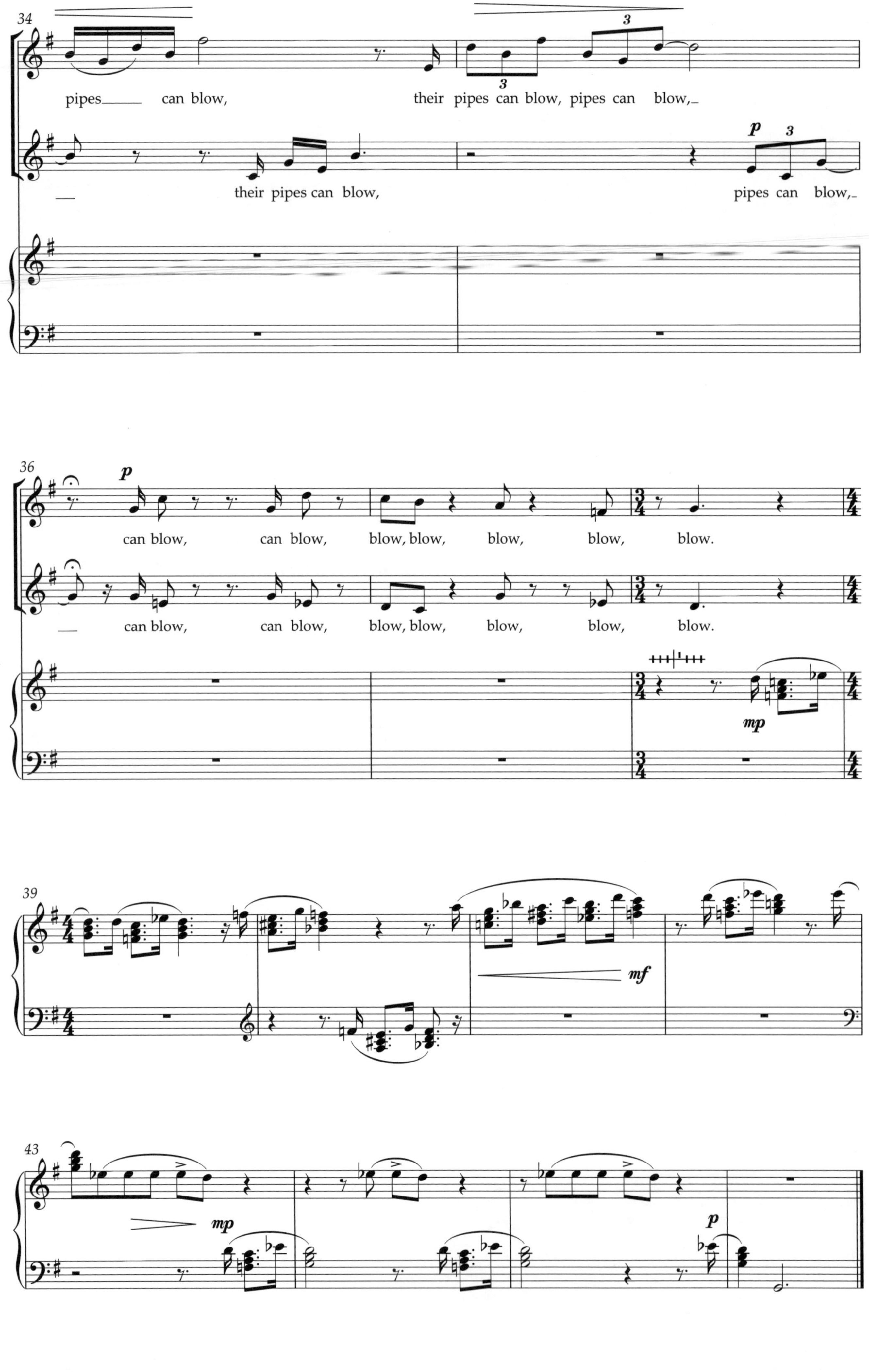

34

pipes___ can blow, their pipes can blow, pipes can blow,_

p

___ their pipes can blow, pipes can blow,_

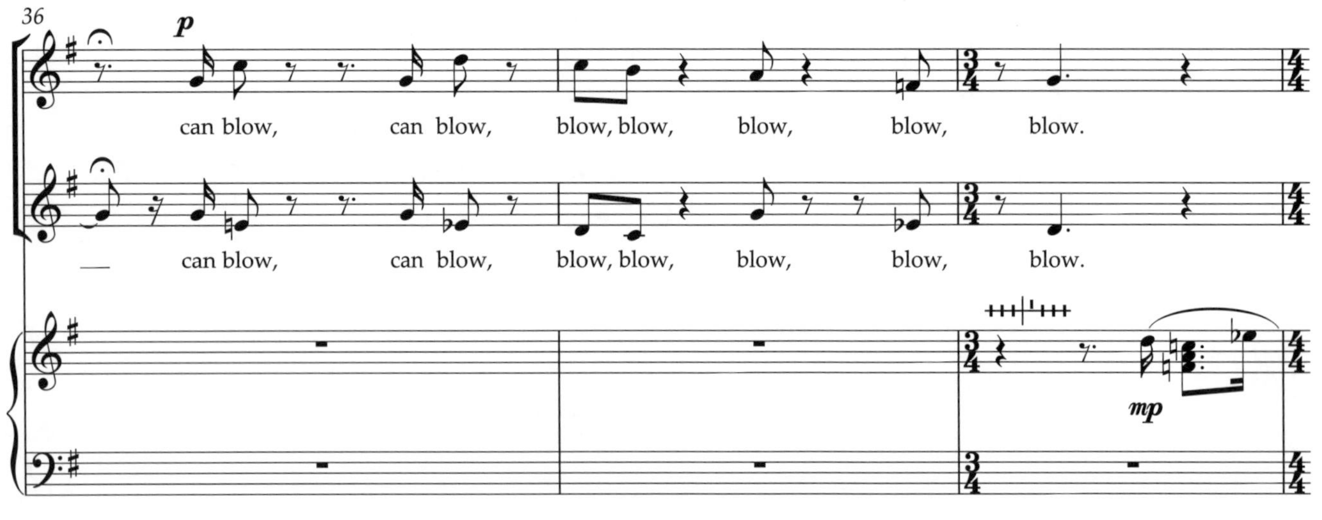
36
p
can blow, can blow, blow, blow, blow, blow, blow.
___ can blow, can blow, blow, blow, blow, blow, blow.
mp

39
mf

43
mp
p